I0759987

Into the Hush

Also by Arthur Sze

POETRY

The Glass Constellation: New and Collected Poems

Sight Lines

Compass Rose

The Ginkgo Light

Quipu

The Redshifting Web: Poems 1970–1998

Archipelago

River River

Dazzled

Two Ravens

The Willow Wind

TRANSLATIONS

The Silk Dragon II: Translations of Chinese Poetry

The Silk Dragon: Translations from the Chinese

EDITOR

Chinese Writers on Writing

INTO THE HUSH

Arthur Sze

Copper Canyon Press
Port Townsend, Washington

Copyright 2025 by Arthur Sze
All rights reserved
Printed in the United States of America

Cover art: Erika Blumenfeld, *Living Light No. 2 (Pyrocystis fusiformis),* detail, 2011.
From the *Bioluminescence* series. www.erikablumenfeld.com

Copper Canyon Press is in residence at Fort Worden State Park in Port Townsend, Washington, under the auspices of Centrum. Centrum is a gathering place for artists and creative thinkers from around the world, students of all ages and backgrounds, and audiences seeking extraordinary cultural enrichment.

LIBRARY OF CONGRESS CATALOGING-IN-PUBLICATION DATA
Names: Sze, Arthur, author.
Title: Into the hush / Arthur Sze.
Description: Port Townsend, Washington : Copper Canyon Press, 2025. |
Summary: "A collection of poems by Arthur Sze"— Provided by publisher.
Identifiers: LCCN 2024036420 (print) | LCCN 2024036421 (ebook) |
ISBN 9781556597145 (hardcover) | ISBN 9781619323148 (epub)
Subjects: LCGFT: Poetry.
Classification: LCC PS3569.Z38 I58 2025 (print) | LCC PS3569.Z38 (ebook) |
DDC 811/.54—dc23/eng/20240823
LC record available at https://lccn.loc.gov/2024036420
LC ebook record available at https://lccn.loc.gov/2024036421

9 8 7 6 5 4 3 2

COPPER CANYON PRESS
Post Office Box 271
Port Townsend, Washington 98368
www.coppercanyonpress.org

for Carol

The poem "Zuihitsu" is published in seven untitled sections interleaved through this book.

Contents

Into the Hush

Anvil

When a black butterfly flits past,

when you glimpse the outlines of apple trees,

when you smell the sprig of sunrise and walk up to the ditch,

when Bering Aleut, Juma, Tuscarora join the list of vanished languages,

when you turn a spigot and irrigate blossoming pear trees,

when the time of your life is a time of earthquakes,

when a woman, hit by a car while crossing the street, recovers then slides into pain,

when a matsutake emerges out of the rubble of Hiroshima,

when a bartender blows smoke rings and slips through hoops into his past,

when foragers slice russulas, amanitas, clitocybes and pursue red-capped boletes,

when water slips through roots, rises through a trunk, streams into leaves,

when in our bodies we sway and flood,

when you bloody your hands,

when the mind like this Earth is struck and tilts its axis,

when, under summer stars, you have built a cabin in the wilderness,

when you gaze at Aldebaran and sense a first frost on the grass,

when in our bodies we ride the waves of our Earth,

here is the anvil on which to hammer your days—

Whoo, whoo. An owl in the tallest blue spruce. Before sunrise. Patches of ice in the driveway.

> *Facing each other, we held a single brush in the air with our right hands. I, left-handed, felt awkward holding it, but, holding it higher up, he beckoned me to start.*

Spring View

I

Listen—in an Anchorage night,
a crunching resembling cars colliding,
and, as the incoming tide slaps,
you will never forget inlet ice breakup;
black spruce branches are etched
against the sky; far from a city lined
with fast-food spots, bars, and pawnshops,
where a siren rises in pitch then ebbs,
you mark galls on young aspen branches;
scale has decimated piñons in the yard;
against this lightening backdrop,
you quicken at a leafing willow,
a magpie stalking in the grass;
you marvel at the green translucency
of leaves, the mystery of photosynthesis;
as grief and joy well up, you step
into the vernal sharpening of the day—
apricot trees are the first to bloom.

2

Forsythia and fire ants emerge—

adjusting the flow of water out of a reservoir—

at a Yucatán airport, a mother retrieves
the body of her scuba-diving son—

"Fucking hell!"

her face flowers in a springtime of grief—

3

Runners in starting blocks
wait for the sound of a gunshot—
a bird warbles, another chitters;
the sky whitens along the ridgeline,

and what in this dawn is yours?
Lichen grips a sandstone wall;
daffodils rise out of the dirt,
brighten in a burst of yellow song;

while the cherry trees bud,
the catalpa appears desiccated
but will leaf just as you despair.
When the pistol fires, the runners

contort in their hundred-yard dash;
in slow motion, their faces
and limbs express a lifetime.
Though a lifetime may be ten seconds,

each second becomes a lifetime
of here, now, be, becoming
yours when you see how
once lines converge, lines diverge.

4

The last speaker of Tehuelche dies—
ants emerge out of a power outlet

and form moving lines; they carry
bits of marrow from a dog bone

on the floor up the cabinet, across
a counter then up the wall into

the opening; they will outlive us all.
The last speaker of Klallam dies—

I weigh, in my mouth, the words
iguanodon, polypropylene,

and guess at the millennia between:
when did the first sycamore

leaf emerge? the first owl?
In Tibet we uncover a fossil

of an arctic fox with razor teeth intact;
you cut and arrange purple lilacs

on the dining table, and when
the aroma pours into the room,

we quicken at this flowering.
How do speakers of Guaraní thrive?

5

$6CO_2 + 6H_2O \xrightarrow[\text{sunlight}]{} C_6H_{12}O_6 + 6O_2$ can't explain it—

water runs in the ditch at 120 gallons per minute—

reverberating sound of a woodpecker—

laughter—

ocean swimming—

when the apple trees bud, a peach tree already blooms—

6

Ice calves off a cliff into the Antarctic—
a magpie nabs a moth off a wall
then lands on a fence post, flips its tail—
a butterfly flits to left, to right,

backward, forward, and points
a way to navigate this world;
but when your body is always rotating,
your center of gravity shifting,

how do you still a butterfly mind?
Who knows the mind of a woman
cleaning houses?—*Fuck,* the owners
are out of town and won't know

if I slip a finger of tequila, sit
in the backyard—I miss the father
of my child—so he had a problem
with *chiva,* held up a jewelry store—

then the car wouldn't start—
he'll be out in five—is there
no end to the pain in my jaw?—
ugh, time to scrub tiles in the shower—

7

A Senegalese fisherman slings an octopus
over his right shoulder and stands near
shore at low tide; along a ski-basin road,
caterpillars emerge and feed on aspen leaves;
in a tropical village, gravediggers cannot
keep up with corpses lined along the road;
into a pot of simmering water, I drop
turkey dumplings, smell traces of ginger,
anticipate a first morsel in my mouth;
when inlet ice crunches in spring breakup,
I instill the flow and grieve at how one man
struggles against another in a spreading oil slick;
it is time to stop tightening the noose
of shrinking habitat around a roaming jaguar,
time to feel sunlight power the air
we breathe; we wake to particles
of burnt wood dropping onto our eyelashes—
saguaros in a canyon explode into flames.

8

When a woman swims in a lake, and evening sunlight bathes grasses along the shore—

when I pulled a blowfish out of the water off Long Island, and it inflated on deck—

when you gather apricots off branches—

when I zigzagged uphill between piñons, listening for a red-tailed hawk—

when sandhill cranes return in low Vs to cornfields at dusk—

when you etched lines into a leaf of an autograph tree—

when we pick cantaloupes out of the garden—

when a kingdom was ruptured yet grasses grew thick—

when we approach a space where lines converge—

when a percussionist held a stick in each hand and struck them in midair—

9

We danced and sang under a canopy during an afternoon shower—

a swallowtail trills its wings as it sips at Russian sage—

sandhill cranes stirred, circled in the air, flew north—

deep and deeper still, into the blue mountains—

that summer evening, we sat in chairs with brightening starlight gaze—

we approach a space where lines touch—

fireflies brightened here, no, there—

sinks a moon to the horizon—

when petals shriveled near a ringer by the front door—

on the roof, the first rain of the year—

A melody played on the piano with five black keys. I heard it, walking across packed snow and ice with microspikes under my shoes.

> *I tried to bring the brush down onto the white paper, but he kept it an inch above. Whiteout. Then we pressed it down and, lifting, completed a dot.*

Among Spruce

Before glimpsing outlines of whorled branches,
you smell spruce needles, know gophers lie

in tunnels belowground, and sense their tracks.
You can't measure the background tracks

of the big bang but believe in finding what
is needed when you must. A sea captain

brewed spruce beer during a voyage and rescued
his crew from scurvy; a famished hiker

consumed spruce needles and emerged out
of the forest. In the darkest minutes before dawn,

you won't ever live to experience pure silence
but were never a composer yearning

for that nirvana. Standing in the cusp of cold,
you hunger for a hummingbird darting from scarlet

penstemon to penstemon in midsummer,
for a shearwater skimming over ocean waves;

now, in this dissolving darkness, you strike
a match and cup this second of warmth, this flame.

Oasis

A tiny spider crawls across the lit screen
of a laptop: what does it make of the world?
Men chisel flagstone and form a stepped patio;
soon a For Sale sign will hang at the street.
Sleeping on my back, I snore then turn
to my side; in the morning you hum before
showering. By afternoon, long lines
of rain vanish before striking the ground,
but we are not distraught; a black morel
rises in a garden; orange blossoming daylilies
arc near a half-spherical stone fountain.
Water murmurs in the basin before it spills
over the edge; before morning spills over
the edge, sunrise makes lakes between clouds.

Dilemma

A musician tumbles bicycle handlebars
        on a sidewalk and makes jangling music;
a gardener prunes branches, then shakes
        the Japanese maple to drop a few

leaves onto the stone path; raking leaves,
        you focus on the noise of the rake;
in a time when pangolins near extinction
        for scales, rhinoceroses for horns,

you find tufts of skunk fur in the grass;
        this is an August with no mushrooms to hunt,
where smoke from the Rio en Medio
        fire stings the eyes; bears swipe suet

from bird feeders, ransack garbage bins
        along streets; and when you drive
to an intersection, a man in a wheelchair
        glares; before turning, you ponder

this chance encounter: as he holds
        an upturned hat and cardboard sign,
War Vet, you wonder, is this truly
        an illusion or an illusion of harrowing truth?

Jaguar Song

—Just after you sign and envision building homes on this tract you smell me in the dark know that I move through this terrain at night   though you only think of building and selling   even now you believe you can borrow my spirit by wearing a mask of my face on your face   look at me   delve into your fears   is your deepest fear to be hacked strangled or be strapped to an IV in a bed with no chance to die   I can grasp a turtle and break its shell with one bite   I can pounce on a deer and crush its skull and neck with my teeth you slash and burn in the jungle   force the snakes and macaws to retreat   you even burn your own species alive   look into my eyes   I am your mirror and transformer   if you destroy my species I will shape-shift and hunt you in your dreams   the fingerprints of your hands resemble the black rosettes on my skin and you will not escape   you will never comprehend the twin nights in my eyes   remember as a child you came up the steps from the basement and flicking off the light at the top of the stairs feared a hand about to grasp your shoulder from behind   that fear is alive   and now as you rummage for keys at your apartment doorstep I am a passing jogger about to pounce   I am the creature who smells your darkest thoughts   and as you turn the key in the lock day or night out of the darkness I spring—

Scintillant

Trudging uphill, I turn onto a deer path
then follow the switchbacks you marked
with orange streamers until I arrive

at a cairn and overlook where I view
the gold run of cottonwoods through the city;
western tanagers migrate through the city.

As I bask in the heat of the afternoon,
I cannot say I had the courage to march
across a bridge and risk being beaten

for the right to vote; at an antiwar rally,
I retreated when police, mounted on horses,
crossed the street with batons swinging.

As I stride down the switchbacks, I can't
put into words the radiance of this day;
I stop at a robin's nest lined with mud

fallen in the grass and scintillate
when at night we step into the yard
and stare up through apple branches at stars.

Full moon. Dogs barking, racing up and down the glassed-in hallway. Xenon, krypton, argon, neon, helium. Inert gases. Blue bottles on branches. Nothing's inert. Where am I?

> *Moving the brush in the air, we made another downward stroke, then, releasing pressure, brought it up. I drew a deep breath—*

Vectors

First extinction in the Galápagos Islands, the least vermilion flycatcher—

Hopis drill a foot deep and plant blue corn along a wash—

Danger, a woman brushed on the side of a napalm bomb—

in an oblong box emptied of firewood, a black-widow web—

shaving, he nicked himself and stared in the mirror in a moment of blood—

out of a saddlebag, a teen pulls a severed goat's head—

before signing his name, he recalls hotel rooms were once used as torture chambers—

in Thessaloníki, the beach attendant made a gun of his hand and fired at him—

prisoners cackled when the inmate onstage said, "Is it not time for my painkiller?"—

weighing mushrooms, the Tibetan cashier grins, "You suffer from suspicion; I suffer
from kindness"—

a mercenary turned car mechanic spilled a pile of Krugerrands onto the table—

looking up from a tusk under the lamp, the carver smiled, "It's butter in my hands"—

Architect's Watercolor

An architect draws a watercolor
depicting two people about to enter
a meeting room, while someone
on the stairway gazes through windows

at a park, river, skyscrapers beyond;
he does not want to be locked
like a carbon atom in a benzene ring
but needs to rotate, lift off,

veer along wharves and shoreline.
In the acoustics of this space,
he catches a needle bounce
off a black granite floor, wanders

from a main walkway, encounters
prickly pear burned purple in wind.
In the ocean gusts before dawn,
he yearns for a Mediterranean spray

where sunlight tingles eyelashes,
where sand releases heat
under the stars. In the atrium,
two violinists launch fireworks

of sound that arc, explode, dissolve
into threads of melodic charm.
Here slate near a pool of water
absorbs sunlight, releases ripples

into the evening; and in this space,
each minute is encounter:
he steps out and makes
footprints on a sidewalk dusted with snow.

Farolitos

We pour sand into brown lunch bags, then place
a votive candle

inside each; at night, lined along the driveway,
the flickering lights

form a spirit way, but what spirit? what way?
We sight the flames

and, swaying within, know the future's fathomless;
we grieve, yearn, joy,

pinpoints in a greater darkness, and spy sunlight
brighten craters

on a half-lit moon; in this life, you may try, try
to light a match, fail,

fail again and again; yet, letting go, you strike
a tip one more time

when it bursts into flame— now the flames
are lights in bags again,

and we glimpse the willow tips clutch at a lunar
promise of spring.

Eraser Song

—Caoutchouc I was named in the Amazon and renamed rubber when a chemist rubbed me against scratchings from a lead pencil today I am composed of volcanic ash held in a vulcanized matrix where my polymers lift the black letters of your graphite off a page when you rub and rub me against black lines you don't recognize I work more by chemical contact than by force when you look at ice crystals glinting in the sun you see white roses dropping white petals onto white paper and as a prism bends sunlight into a spectrum of colors joy widens into a delta of joys you don't notice all the letters of all the words you discard ravel off me they sting just as your eyes sting when you gaze into fresh sunlit snow when you look at *th q ck br wn f x j mp d v r th l zy d g* and find I've lifted all the vowels loss quickens the world when a cloud passes across the sun and the sun reappears you register how vanished lines and lines on a page form a palimpsest when you coalesce your words to reclaim *the quick brown fox jumped over the lazy dog* you recognize we need each other and while my gift is that all the letters of all the words you discard smudge off me your secret is that all those letters amass like a glowing white Pyramid of Giza in the night desert behind your eyes—

Dawn Branches

Owls hoot back and forth—

inside a pencil, *peace*
waits to be written—

gunshots, blood cries in streets—

shouts ricochet
in November moonlight—

this is not about last things—

drawing a curve, he sees the graphite erode:
he can never make an unending circle—

this is about anticipation,

your time on this planet,
this stark branch, sapphire light, steel rake noise—

this fern leaf ooze compressed—

these carbonized
griefs and hungers—

lifting sounds
out of the cauldron of silence—

branches of a golden rain tree emerge out of darkness—

Drought

Deer raise their ears, as he steps on gravel, then lower their heads and browse on grass, as he moves beyond them toward the street. He does not know why the catalpa tree is the first to shed leaves, the last to leaf, but when he stops to gaze up at the bare branches, the sky's a surface of a pond starting to freeze. He has tried and failed, tried and failed all summer; now the garden's overgrown with weeds; another apricot twig snaps when bent; after a rat burrowed into the outdoor sofa, he had it hauled to the dump. In the dark, a gleaming flatbed truck transports large cylinders of waste down a mesa, along city limits, to an underground salt bed. At three a.m., while he sleeps, "Holy shit!" erupts out a doorway; flames rise in an apartment complex, and alarms sound.

Reddening pear leaves—
opening spigots, he drains
the last drops from tanks—

Downwind

When the air clears after days of smoke,
you yearn to swim in an alpine lake
that mirrors clouds and wash the scent
of burned pines from your hair;
from the west, smoke has traveled
a thousand miles, the point of ignition
where a pine snapped a transmission line.

When the air clears after days of smoke,
you notice the serrated edges along
apple leaves, locate a point of ignition
in a word, a jab: a man chalks
a cue stick and, slamming the white ball
into a pyramid of balls, feels for a millisecond
a point of ignition and surge in the clatter.

When the air clears after days of smoke,
you believe you were simply a casualty
downwind, but, as you hold
a Rubik's Cube of time in your hands,
the orange sunrise is nowhere,
everywhere, and—damn—the pieces
are pieces you cannot flip back.

in the beginning, I liked the sounds of *metempsychosis, jazz, cooler,* and did not know that words would guide me, under the bluest sky, to where a single wedge of geese caught the low sunlight with wings, to you—

we leaned the brush horizontally below the dot. When we reached the corner—

Into the Hush

1

A magpie feather gleams in the grass;
today you are not having open-heart surgery,
nor are you strapped to a hospital bed,
inhaling oxygen; you do not mix cement
and sand in a wheelbarrow, nor did you sleep
the night in a field off an interstate highway.
This morning you live in a sparrow's warble,
in pale green leaves trembling in sunshine.
You catch the curling wave of the day
where peas flower on a trellis, where apricot
blossoms tinge the tips of a hundred-year-old tree.
Weeding in the garden, you get stronger
as you dig; you become well, island, field;
out of nowhere, a rough-legged hawk
glides downward with outstretched wings;
aspen leaves flutter without wind. When you've
worked this long, your art is no longer art
but a wand that wakes your eyes to what is.

2

Purple irises about to unfurl—

he tries to stain the sanded redwood deck,
but cottonwood tufts land everywhere—

smell of bread rising from a basement oven—

gold earrings on a bedside table—

a cloud passes across the sun and darkens the brick—

when *is* is becoming—

digging a trench for a new waterline,
he shovels a blue bottle up into daylight—

as a supermoon drops to the horizon—

3

Lichens on a bridge absorb truck fumes;
larger than Manhattan, an iceberg
calves off the Antarctic shelf;
a man at a gas station opens fire on others.

In the dark, you can't see coyotes
beyond the fence but hear them gather;
a skater leaps into a triple lutz
then slips on landing; a dog trots

up with a headless raven in its mouth.
As a hawk glides over a canyon
with outstretched wings, you scan for movement;
titanium scraps dumped into a barrel

of radioactive waste start sparking;
something starts sparking inside you.
Walking on a sheet of ice over a lake,
you sense the edge of danger

changing shape underneath; literal facts
of this world tighten in a noose;
a swift stays airborne for months,
while a flicker sips water pooled on a tarp.

4

On a ladder, lifting a nest off a beam,
I find dried mud at the base;
inside are no eggs or parts of shell:
the matted, circular interior
contrasts with the skewed stalks
of the exterior where, in a flurry of wings,
a sparrow bled, and two crows

feasted on eggs. I have no wings
or winged sandals, am no guide
to the realm of the dead,
but, basking in this June light,
I hear a neighbor's chain saw run
all afternoon against an elm by the street
and wince, let go, wince, let go;

then, mycorrhizal, as mind and nature
entwine each other, and as a skater
gathers speed, I lift off the ice,
not knowing if I will fail
or land, but, in the spin of a leap,
lift in the risk of what we may become,
and find a daylight inside day.

5

The peyote plant in this pot has not shifted hue
or grown the slightest; month after month,
staring at the crown, I yearn for a bud,
but none appears, and its blue-slate hue
is like gazing down a clouded gravel road
at dusk; yet, in this ocotillo moment,
I smell how this place craves rain.
A woodpecker has drilled holes into a piñon trunk,
and I write into the hush: at dawn, as outlines
of a Japanese maple emerge out of darkness,
the black branches of an alligator juniper
with sky whitening behind, I write along
the curve of an expanding wave that delineates
the shapes of all things. Near the front door,
I snap the twig of a lavender bush;
as a hunter of a gemsbok runs for hours
in the gait of a gemsbok, in spring I want
to take on the contours of spring before stepping out:

6

out of the blue of a robin's eggs—

out of the abyss when a cellist pauses between notes—

out of the semaphore of saying something we did not know we knew—

out of an Olmec dagger unearthed when digging a new subway line—

out of all seasons at once—

praise to finding a single black morel in a cardiologist's garden—

to aspen leaves motionless after rain—

to finding a rotating lighthouse beam when waves crashed against our vessel under
    lightning-filled clouds—

to the lichen green with wavy edges on a wet, black trunk—

to the sunlight we awaken in each other—

praise to the white balls of viburnum that effloresce and drop to the ground—

to the gold shower when a violinist's bow runs against strings—

to the radiating joy grief despair hope love that make us human—

to the patter of rain on the roof before sunrise—

to daylight that is daylight—

to the hush that is now—

clink: we sipped champagne out of handblown Venetian glass flutes, spread black caviar on blinis—glimmering ice, glimmering water—dot, months of dots, years, dragons, ink smeared, splattered on rice paper with a cap—ha!—dragon after dragon in mist and roiling water—

I tried to angle it downward to the left, but, resisting the motion that was supposed to be a continuation of a single stroke, he paused:

Užupis

Passing an accordion player in the street,
            I mark a building, with names and dates
carved into the fitted blocks of a wall,

            whose former basement prison is open
to visitors. In the adjacent park,
            two women greet each other and hug.

The smoke of the past seeps into my clothes;
            when an invisible cloud of radioactive dust
settled on spruce and birch forests,

            foragers picked and dined on mushrooms
only to wake, convulse, die.
            As I walk over a bridge, spot

empty picture frames dangling below,
            a bench swing suspended over rushing water,
I wonder, what is the swing of destiny?

            In this city armies have marched through,
from the east, from the west, from the east,
            I sip a salty mineral water laced

with calcium, magnesium, sulfates,
            while others fill bottles, chug.
Standing in a district that declares itself

            a republic inside a city, whose last article
of Dada constitution says, Do not surrender,
            I swing out of myself on invisible wings.

Río Chamita

Mule deer browse in the meadow
    and meander in clusters down the slope
        across a dry pond bed;

at a shooting range, we stare at a machine
  loaded with orange-centered circular targets

        but are not here to practice firing at ducks;

you climb a metal ladder, sit
  on a bench high in a ponderosa pine,

    and, gazing far, say *hunters shoot from here;*

we step onto a floating dock, while swallows
    scissor the air, loop back,

        fuchsia-streaked clouds undulating on water;

and when we canoed around a floating island of reeds,
  I understood we came here
        to ignite behind our eyelids—

a yellow-headed blackbird perches on a cattail;
        beyond a green metal fence, buffalo graze—

while water runs into this pond, before it spills
    over a metal gate into the Río Chamita,

            we gather our lives in this pooling—

Winter Solstice

My shadow lengthens in the driveway—
        this morning I was going to repair
the slanting posts to that split-rail fence;
        instead I scanned through binoculars

for an indigo bunting—now a gathering
        darkness constricts what I can do;
in the little daylight left, I grieve
        that I attended to things that had

no sliver of success: if I spotted
        a bunting at a feeder, would it have—
blue, blue deepening then rising
        into quetzal green—flared me

before it vanished? When I stop luring
        a flash of success, misfortune
will stop pursuing me; now I stand
        near a bonfire in the street, warming

my hands and face, but my feet
        in boots numb; I think, no, I should say
I am thought; the yellow sunlight
        grows hair, the black leopard

of night cracks a fibula in its maw;
        and when the North Pole reaches
its farthest point, what if that distance
        seizes and sizzles into a habit of mind?

Papyrus Pantoum

Coyotes surround a buck   staggering in the snow—
under a rising moon, we step   along a ridge of white sand;

sandhill cranes return in low Vs   and land in a cornfield—
in Bolivia, they extract   lithium out of Altiplano salt flats;

under a rising moon,   we step along a ridge of white sand—
"You burn me"   torn off papyrus wrapped around a corpse;

in Bolivia, they extract lithium   out of Altiplano salt flats—
a claret cup cactus flowers   among sandstone rubble;

"You burn me" torn   off papyrus wrapped around a corpse—
rain makes quicksilver   strikes on the surface of a lake;

a claret cup cactus   flowers among sandstone rubble—
in twilight, we sway   and surge into flame;

rain makes quicksilver strikes   on the surface of a lake—
coyotes surround   a buck staggering in the snow;

in twilight, we sway and surge   into flame—
sandhill cranes return   in low Vs and land in a cornfield.

Swimming Laps

Swimming backstroke toward the far end of a pool in sunlight—

yellow flares in the nearby aspens—

in the predawn sky, Mars and Venus glimmered—

how is it a glimmering moment coalesces, and the rest slides like flour
through a sieve?—

how is it these glimmerings become constellations in a predawn sky?—

reaching the wall, I turn and push off swimming freestyle—

how is it we bobbed in water beyond the breaking surf, and I taste that salt
in my mouth now?—

how is it, disheveled, breathless, we drew each other up into flame?—

how is it that flame burns steadily within?—

reaching the wall, I turn and push off swimming sidestroke—

with each scissors kick, I know time's shears—

this is not predawn to a battle when the air dips to a windless calm—

let each day be lived risking feeling loving alive to ivy reddening along the fence—

reaching the wall, I turn and push off swimming breaststroke—

how is it I see below then above a horizon line?—

how is it I didn't sputter, slosh, end up staring at a Geiger-counter clock
mounted on a barroom wall?—

I who have no answers find glimmering shards—

reaching the wall, I pause, climb out of the pool, start a new day—

Shadows of Flames

Juniper crackles,   and piñon smoke scents the room;
bins of coriander, cumin, red chile powder,   fenugreek—

at a keyhole entrance,   we gaze into the garden of the Taj;
bomb warnings   pasted on glass doors and on walls;

bins of coriander,   cumin, red chile powder, fenugreek;
shadows of flames wash   across our bodies—

bomb warnings pasted on glass doors   and on walls;
bar-tailed godwits   fly eight thousand miles before stopping—

shadows of flames   wash across our bodies—
small circles, large circles,   circumference is everywhere;

bar-tailed godwits fly   eight thousand miles before stopping—
quicksilver lightning, peony moon,   this kiss;

small circles, large circles, circumference   is everywhere;
at a keyhole entrance, we gaze   into the garden of the Taj;

quicksilver lightning,   peony moon, this kiss;
juniper crackles, and piñon smoke   scents the room—

Letter to Tao Qian

I wish to tell you but lose the words—
        more than a millennium later,
on another continent, in another language,
        I know adversity strengthened you.

Today we possess antibiotics,
        cars, cell phones; scientists
use infrared scanners, check a wildfire
        that has charred 341,735 acres.

When you picked chrysanthemums
        by the bamboo fence to the east,
then gazed at mountains to the south,
        at birds homing at sunset,

you turned in three directions,
        centering yourself; though you omitted north,
I posit *mortality* as you sipped wine.
        Today we have no spell

that lessens loss; a neighbor's backhoe
        beeps as it excavates a slope.
Sifting your words, I dig at this site
        where pines scent after rain;

a black swallowtail lands
        on Russian sage, bending the stalk;
as it imbibes nectar and sways, I sway;
        light slants all that we do.

tennis players ran left and right, hitting forehands, backhands; as one player raced up to the net, the other lobbed—around Earth, 35,000 pieces of shrapnel each larger than a tennis ball circled at 17,500 miles per hour—

angling the brush down, we completed roof, *added two dots, then,*
below, swung it, horizontally, from left to right. Lifting—

Forage

I The Shore of This Day

You walk on a path lined with palm fronds,
and mosquitoes swarm, but no, not yet—
once, before you stepped into a rainforest,
a cloud of mosquitoes rose in the clearing;
when the cloud dissipated, you headed
to a temple where you climbed the steps,
and reaching the pinnacle, surveying
a canopy of ceiba trees, saw other temples
overrun by vegetation. That night, noises
in the rainforest were raspings on guiros—
you saw mosquitoes swarm a bloated
body floating on a lake; and in the morning,
when you walked out of that rainforest,
bitten alive, you walked out of a past life.
In the coos of this morning's white-winged dove,
sounds of howler monkeys reach
the shore of this day: you step onto an island,
walk on a path lined with palm fronds.

2 Oxbow Lakes

Quartz, peak, crowd, junk, tiger, rose—
the audiologist asks me to repeat
the last word to each sentence,
while she slowly turns up background
noise until it obliterates language.
As I listen, a plume of water
laden with tritium seeps,
under a mesa, into an aquifer;
in Point Barrow, polar bears
rummage through trash at the city dump;
as I listen, an Iñupiat woman
steps out of her apartment, avoids
needles scattered in the parking lot.
I say *witness* and recognize,
against noise, consciousness
as a river that floods, shortens course,
leaving behind oxbow lakes;
and, in this immediate time,
when I say *convolution,*
we can land a probe on a comet
but can't end hunger across the street.

3 Forage

In the night, a black bear climbs a pear tree,
snaps branches, feasts on pears in the grass;
one night you turned onto a dead-end street

and—*click click click click*—in your headlights,
two guys, stripping wheels off a car
jacked up on blocks, turned and fled.

You glimpsed their faces; at the post office,
the clerk has a face like sunlight that dims
then brightens as he ticks a countdown

to retirement; when he reaches zero,
will white spikes precipitate out of solution?
Will he detonate? You precipitate

a migraine when you walk office corridors all day;
a lawyer says he will write a great American
novel when he takes leave from work next year;

next year is a beach vacation in Samoa;
in kindergarten, a child draws a gorilla on roller skates—
in a lifetime, when do a child's dreams ignite?

4 Divagation

Under stars, listening to a coloratura soprano,
    he looks at glimmering lights on a mesa
where suited technicians use gloved hands
    inside sealed boxes to assemble pits

for W88 warheads. As he watches,
    twenty-one miles to the north, three men
smoke crack, abduct a woman, inject
    her with heroin, push her over a bridge

into the Rio Grande. And as she floats
    to shore, he floats to shore, rises out
of the muck, in drenched jeans and T-shirt,
    mouth bloodied, staggers, shivering,

to a lit house and finds no one's unscathed.
    Sparkling *Ah*s and *Hell's vengeance*
erupt in starbursts under an August sky;
    though people shout, in silence

he stands at a construction site, where
    he lasts only a morning, as a foreman
hands him a sledgehammer and, leaning
    on a block wall, says, *Start swinging, start here.*

5 Floaters

Driving past a phalanx of white tombstones
          along a south-facing slope,

I recall, "No one hates war like soldiers,"
          from a mechanic replacing

an oil pump in a Fiat engine; then another floater
          appears when I blink—

peach blossoms on flowing water go
          into the distance—

and, as I ponder how a line written in 740
          stays present tense—

a curve-billed thrasher nests in a cleft of spined cholla—
          a man, on ayahuasca,

types with his hands, and his hands disappear;
          he types with his hands,

and his hands disappear—shimmer the words
          as his hands disappear.

6 Wildfire Season

The wind stokes flames,
and they leap across
the fire line; to the north,

a jagged red-and-yellow
ridgeline crackles
with billowing clouds of smoke.

To the far north, a singer
stretches walrus bladder
and, completing a box drum,

starts to hum; he nods
as a song takes shape in his hands.
The smallest

subatomic particles trace
the birth of the cosmos;
traces of scorpion venom

will lead to new cures;
one day they will extract
heavy metals from the moon.

The spider in a sink
sips from a droplet of water;
leaf-cutter ants

will one day march
across a radioactive forest.
In this wind,

pear trees unfold white blossoms,
shape a song as
time detonates inside of time.

7 Against the Rubble

Nature loves to hide—
stopping on a trail
I spot a horned lizard

that, stilled near my shoes,
against the rubble
of sandstone and quartz,

blends in; heading uphill
I mark a budding
pincushion cactus

and tips of piñons
greener after rain—
the green of trinitite

holds a trace of the tower;
an observer remarked
the heat, at twelve miles—

before I reach the run
of pinecones down a slope,
a coyote, head turned,

tail bobbing, traverses ahead—
was like opening
a 500-degree oven—

below the overlook I stop
where someone set
rocks in a semicircle,

and, cupping my hands over
invisible flames,
gaze up at black black stars.

8 Floaters

Magpies fly from branch to branch. In the slow
tide of the afternoon, you sleep in my arms;
we drift to shore, as sea turtles beach;

the ocean surf breaks; an incoming
wave foams up on sand then subsides.
Stepping into daylight after weeks of smoke,

we smell rain before it begins to rain;
in the open garage, we exude an aroma
of juniper bark, roll a Ping-Pong table

into place, and, lowering the legs, stretch
the net, volley. Sending a white ball
back and forth, back and forth, we sway

in season. Now we stride into a sloping lava tube,
and water drips in the dark. As we emerge
into rainforest, an ʻapapane flits

among branches; sunlight dapples our eyelids;
we follow a path that splits into many
paths as leaves on ʻōhiʻa trees shimmer.

9 Midsummer

Tiger swallowtails hover over Russian sage—
I smell eucalyptus where there is no
eucalyptus and locate summer in rain.
Like bats emerging out of a cave at dusk,
a thread of grief unfurls in the sky.
Neither you nor I can stop the planting
of mines in a field or the next detonation.
I unclog a drip line along a fence;
in May, lilacs arced over the road in a cascade
of purple blossoms. Now, stilled in a minute
of darkness, I listen to bamboo leaves
unfurl above into sunshine. Untangling
a necklace composed of interlocking
gold chains, then lifting it, I trace
joy, fear, bewilderment, bliss, a *this*
resplendent in my fingertips. I slip inside
a strawberry runner that extends root, leaf,
then stand in morning starlight and inhabit a song.

hiking a trail along the Nāpali Coast—our bodies, brushes—we stopped at Hanakāpīʻai Beach and swam out beyond the breakers; later, we learned of twenty drownings—

> *we brought it vertically down below the horizontal line, ran it from left to right; then I gasped, gasped at* emptiness—

Leafless

Sunlight strikes the leafless aspen branches,
strikes the white picket fence, and as I
look at highlighted edges, my eyes sting.
Tufted grass stalks sway in the flooding rays,
and, in the poinsettia of this hour, I need
some darkness to bloom: in this space
a snow leopard leaps among rocks,
the rosettes of its fur a moving landscape;
its hunger scents the air. As I exhale,
a blue-throated hillstar sips from a chuquiragua
flower, a fly agaric pushes out of soil,
a raccoon scampers backward down an elm—
we are always running from and lunging to;
when we stop, the eagle feather
of this pause blesses. Before light
of the shortest day lifts to the hills,
it runs across my line of sight in widening gold.

Morning Mist

1

Mist veils the apricot branches and trunks—
magpies and crows spread across the grass in silence—

2

White flags run uphill
from the street to a neighbor's construction site—

in this near distance, the flags are tiny flags of surrender—

3

No one can see a line that divides "ours" from "theirs"—
no one shouts, whines, or threatens—

4

Looking at the lines in his palms, he does not prognosticate
but sees a history of struggle—

along the sloping driveway,
a cluster of daffodil shoots—

5

As he inhales, gratitude runs through his fingers—
exhaling, he notices mailboxes on posts—

6

Remnants of hail, white, over grass—
sunlight comes and sounds like copper chimes—

Architectures of Emptiness

1

Yogis call these buoyed minutes
the moment of the universe, and who knows
if spruce, aspen, and a golden rain tree
converse, like mycelium, through roots?
As pink limns the black ridgeline, you hear
a ruby-crowned kinglet but can't see
if it is nestled in a fir or alligator juniper;
will another summer of crackling fires stench the air?
Will tent caterpillars infest the cottonwood?
Will an orange sunrise sting your eyes,
as helicopters dump liquid fertilizer
onto thousands of acres of burning conifers?
An architect dynamites rock to create
a skylight for a cliffside dwelling that,
below ground, has three rock walls
and one glassed-in side—though we come
and go like streamers of yellowing forsythia—
that looks toward sunrise over a white-capping sea.

2

Clearing twigs and branches, shoveling silt,

> *—one monk scrapes*
> *a knuckle through sand,*

we chop willow shoots rising out of the acequia;

> *makes a gray X;*
> *then another,*

on a post, a spotted towhee rotates its head,

> *holding a paintbrush,*
> *sweeps the colored sands*

sideways, up, down, before flying off;

> *from perimeter to center;*
> *another collects them*

I pause at these minute shifts—

> *in an urn;*
> *then they disperse the sands*

in the predawn dark, I am infinitesimal

> *on flowing water, laying out,*
> *in minute detail*

gazing up at Deneb but brighten as the sky

> *the palace and ephemerality*
> *of all endeavors:*

brightens and see our lives unfurl:

> *what is stilled flows,*
> *what is destroyed liberates—*

3

For each holder of water rights,
days and times start
at the lowest elevation
then move upstream
toward the reservoir.
On the first day, water
soaks the length
of the ditch and clears silt;
soon sedge, wax currant,
thinleaf alder sprout.
We divert water into downhill
pipes that run to drip lines
and rotating sprinklers:
sprigs of apricots flower;
catkins burst; I pace
our length, clear debris,
scan for cyanic milkvetch,
tufted sand verbena,
Springer's blazing star.
We have that western
wheatgrass, this wire rush,
and scratch—match
to flame—a path of
devotion into empty space.

4

Mark the shadows of aspen leaves
        rippling on grass; beneath a veil
of white bark, aspens have a photosynthetic
        layer that absorbs sunlight

through winter; a magpie sails
        across a yard, flutters wing feathers,
and, landing on spruce, squawks—
        it speaks to you; thin-leaf alder

shoots rising out of the ditch speak;
        you stand in Tree pose: inhale,
exhale, *inhale, exhale:* water
        is to emptiness as sun is to language;

you sluice into the infinite tangle
        of beginnings and ends: cottonwood
seeds swirl in the air; a wild
        apricot blooms by the ditch; suddenly

each aspen leaf on a tree is a word,
        the movement of leaves their syntax:
burns   diamond light diffuse it
        so   we   green green,

diamond light burns so we
        diffuse it into greening—
suddenly you parse the leaves,
        and they are speaking to you now:

Fugitive

Red begonias stricken by frost—

listen: they nail plywood sheets and complete the garage decking—

swarmed by mosquitoes, you wander hot, thirsty, disoriented in a palm forest—

you have bloodied your hands on barbed wire—

after a snowfall, you inhale starlight while standing in an orchard—

you have had three operations to repair a torn elbow—

green mist rising from leafing willows—

running across a dune of white sand, you discover a pile of oryx bones—

they stack elephant tusks in a pyramid and set them on fire—

you have staggered out of a house in flames and lived to say this—

you have been thrust by rifle butt to a river and heard someone shout, "Swim!"—

the grass turns to yellow-gold stalks—

minutes replete with the noise of honeybees—

minutes replete with river gold—

asleep, she rides the waves of her breath onto the shore of your shoulder—

you coil hoses and haul them to a barn—

you have loved, hated, imagined, despaired, and the fugitive colors of existence
    have quickened in your body—

after seventy years, you write with shivering memory into the sunrise—

Venn Diagrams

X-rays, muons, ultraviolet radiation—
X-rays can diagnose fractures
in the skull; muons can map spaces
inside the pyramids at Giza;
ultraviolet radiation kills bacteria
in well water—in a Venn diagram,
circles overlap. An array of sharpened
pencils in a cup; cars parked
at a casino; along a trail, small
puffballs—these clusters manifest
chance; and, pondering three
who furthered you on your way,
you grieve, yearn, hope, make lines
against a void, *the* void, in an at-one-go.

Pe'ahi Light

I

Half-filled with sand, a Karatsu teabowl
placed on a writing desk: no incense

smokes the air; above, on a wall, *heart,*
brushed in three strokes, where the black

ends of each stroke flare into the void.
We zigzagged across a dry streambed;

that night, a breeze surged like incoming surf—
waves of rain crashed, subsided, plunged;

now, in Pe'ahi light, rain patters the fronds,
glistens the fishtail palms, the stilt root palms,

the white elephant palm, butterfly palm,
a palm, twenty inches tall, risen out

of a split coconut. *Drizzle, rain, downpour*—
I have no words for these kinds of rain;

I mark a conch shell doorstop, a dictionary
of etymology: *rain,* from Old English,

regn—a frond emerges out of the dark—
rain stops, water beads at the tips of ferns.

2

Geckos click and squiggle up a windowpane;
crisscrossing palm fronds and blades

of sunlight block lines of sight; when a frond
sways, you sway, tingling in yellow light,

arched forty feet above ground; when
a frond stills, you still, mark a spray of red ginger.

On another continent, a man lies strapped
to a hospital bed and can't rampage

across a room he no longer recognizes.
Before opening a window, you pause

at desiccated geckos caught between a screen
and windowpane. Are we ensnared

by hazards we cannot comprehend?
A feral chicken clucks below the house.

You spy a Tahitian lime on a branch, another
yellowing farther up. On a far shore,

two women shriek as one reels in a silver
fish that bounces along the surface of lake water.

3

Sitting on a round blue cushion in a room
with three white walls, where a fourth

has screened glass doors that open
onto a lanai, I focus on the spackled

ceiling and, finding contours of mesas
and arroyos from the air, know I overlay

these shapes onto emptiness. As warm air
flows in, I smell clusters of white ginger

flowering below; earlier, we walked
a trail down a bluff to where Papalua Stream

empties into Pilale Bay and saw divers
out among white-capping waves. Did they

dive for reef triggerfish? Octopi? In the space
of not-knowing, I ~~float~~ joy when

the ~~body~~ mind unfolds and ~~tolls~~ flowers
from inside the ~~bell~~ gong of silence,

and I spark when ~~language~~ love~~—*1457,*
sudden unexpected attack or capture—~~surprises.

4

Facing east, blue lions flank the front door—
a machete, hat, compass, splintered

ukulele mounted on a wall quiet
this room; on a desk, a globe maps

the world known to Europeans in 1745;
today we can map the fractal

contours of a coastline, but what's
never obsolete is the unappeasable urge

to speak. A couple hikes a switchback
trail down to the bay; sitting in the shade,

we overhear, "*Fuck* this, *fuck* that,"
some stomping, then they disappear.

An impoverishment of language's
an impoverishment of life; we want

to see the empty sky fly into pieces,
to incorporate three systoles

in writing *heart* and bloom
through lifetimes within a single lifetime.

5

Carols an ʻamakihi in the forest after a shower—
the pendant lobster claws of a heliconia

gleam in sunlight amid a green thicket of leaves.
This morning we bobbed in ocean waves,

swam in sight of an island with a single palm
at the summit, observed flat-bottomed,

cumulus-topped, steel-blue clouds sail
low over water, listened to surf break

over black lava rock, over black lava rock;
scanning the horizon's curving rim,

I yearned to see a pod of humpback whales,
but, through binoculars, saw an endless

shimmer of wave crests that stung my eyes.
Now, as a gecko darts across eucalyptus flooring,

as I strive to make a poem that scintillates
in the dark, scintillates in the dark,

we do not stagger, zombie-zapped,
but spark in our bodies glistening in misting rain.

Acknowledgments

Grateful acknowledgment is made to the editors of the following publications in which these poems appeared, sometimes in earlier versions:

Acanto (Portugal): "Oasis," "Papyrus Pantoum," and sections 7–9 of "Spring View" (reprints)

The Adroit Journal: "Oasis"

The Atlantic: "Floaters" (Magpies fly . . .)

The Baffler: "Divagation"

Big Other: "Scintillant"

Conjunctions: "Architectures of Emptiness," "Dawn Branches," and "Eraser Song"

Domus (Italy): "Architect's Watercolor," "Downwind," "Oasis," and "Río Chamita" (reprints)

Freeman's: The Best New Writing on Animals: "Oxbow Lakes"

The Georgia Review: "Spring View"

Harper's Magazine: "Drought," "Užupis," and "Winter Solstice"

Harvard Review: "Wildfire Season"

High Country News: "Morning Mist"

The Kenyon Review: "Into the Hush" and "Letter to Tao Qian"

Lana Turner: "Shadows of Flames"

Literary Hub: "Among Spruce"

Michigan Quarterly Review Online: "Jaguar Song" and "Río Chamita"

The New Yorker: "Anvil," "Farolitos," "Fugitive," "Swimming Laps," and "Vectors"

The New York Review of Books: "Against the Rubble"

The Paris Review: "Dilemma" and "Zuihitsu"

Plume: "Venn Diagrams"

Poetry: "Architect's Watercolor," "Floaters" (Driving past . . .), section 3 of "Forage," "Midsummer," "Papyrus Pantoum," "Pe'ahi Light," and "The Shore of This Day"

Poetry Sky: "Among Spruce," "Architect's Watercolor," "Dawn Branches," and "Swimming Laps" (reprints)

Terrain.org: "Downwind"

The Yale Review Poem of the Week: "Leafless"

The Best American Poetry 2023, edited by Elaine Equi and David Lehman (Scribner, 2023): "Wildfire Season"

The Best American Poetry 2024, edited by Mary Jo Salter and David Lehman (Scribner, 2024): "Pe'ahi Light"

In the American Grain, edited by Claudia Laganà (UK, Europe Books, 2022): "Río Chamita"

Leaning toward Light: Poems for Gardens & the Hands That Tend Them, edited by Tess Taylor (Storey Publishing, 2023): "Oasis"

New Mexico Poetry Anthology 2023, edited by Levi Romero and Michelle Otero (Museum of New Mexico Press, 2023): "Farolitos"

Poets in Conversation: Asia Speaks, edited by Eddie Tay and Jenny Wong (UK, Out-Spoken Press, 2023): "Letter to Tao Qian"

Sign & Breath: Voice & the Literary Tradition, edited by Philip Brady and Shanta Lee Gander (Etruscan Press, 2024): "Swimming Laps"

I thank the poets, writers, and architect who published these poems: Peter LaBerge, David Barber, J.W. McCormack, John Madera, Bradford Morrow, John Freeman, Gerald Maa, Ben Lerner, Chloe Garcia Roberts, Major Jackson, Christina Thompson, Paisley Rekdal, Nicole Terez Dutton, David Baker, Calvin Bedient, David Lau, Khaled Mattawa, Kevin Young, Hannah Aizenman, Jana Prikryl, Vijay Seshadri, Emily Nemens, Emily Stokes, Daniel Lawless, Su Cho, Esther Belin, Adrian Matejka, Simmons Buntin, Derek Sheffield, Meghan O'Rourke,

Maggie Millner, Maria Celeste Alves, Elaine Equi, Mary Jo Salter, David Lehman, Steven Holl, Claudia Laganà, Tess Taylor, Levi Romero, Michelle Otero, Yidan Han, Jenny Wong, Eddie Tay, Philip Brady, and Shanta Lee Gander.

Thanks to Forrest Gander and to Jane Hirshfield. And thanks to Jim Moore and Carol Moldaw for reading drafts of these poems.

Thank you, Michael Wiegers, for your unflagging support of my work through the years, and thanks to Ryo Yamaguchi, Ashley E. Wynter, Claretta Holsey, and everyone at Copper Canyon Press.

"Pe'ahi Light" was written while I was an artist in residence at the Merwin Conservancy on Maui, from July to August 2022. Thanks to Sonnet Coggins and Sara Tekula.

I am grateful for the 2021 Shelley Memorial Award from the Poetry Society of America and for a 2022 Ruth Lilly Poetry Prize from the Poetry Foundation, which were a great help in writing this book.

About the Author

Arthur Sze is the twenty-fifth poet laureate of the United States and author of twelve books of poetry, including *The Glass Constellation: New and Collected Poems* (2021), selected for a 2024 National Book Foundation Science + Literature Prize; *Sight Lines* (2019), for which he received the National Book Award; *Compass Rose* (2014), a Pulitzer Prize finalist; *The Ginkgo Light* (2009), selected for the PEN Southwest Book Award and the Mountains & Plains Independent Booksellers Association Book Award; *Quipu* (2005); *The Redshifting Web: Poems 1970–1998* (1998), selected for the Balcones Poetry Prize and the Asian American Literary Award; and *Archipelago* (1995), selected for an American Book Award. He has also published *The Silk Dragon II: Translations of Chinese Poetry* (2024) and edited *Chinese Writers on Writing* (2010). Another collection, *The White Orchard: Selected Interviews, Essays, and Poems,* was published by the Museum of New Mexico Press in spring 2025.

A recipient of the 2024 Rebekah Johnson Bobbitt National Prize for Poetry, the Ruth Lilly Poetry Prize, the Shelley Memorial Award, the Jackson Poetry Prize, a Lannan Literary Award, a Guggenheim Fellowship, a Lila Wallace–Reader's Digest Writers' Award, two National Endowment for the Arts Creative Writing Fellowships, and a Howard Foundation Fellowship, as well as five grants from the Witter Bynner Foundation for Poetry, Sze was the first poet laureate of Santa Fe, where he lives with his wife, the poet Carol Moldaw. A chancellor emeritus of the Academy of American Poets and a fellow of the American Academy of Arts and Sciences, he was the 2023–2024 Mohr Visiting Poet at Stanford University. His poetry has been translated into fifteen languages, including Chinese, Dutch, German, Portuguese, and Spanish. He is a professor emeritus at the Institute of American Indian Arts.

POETS FOR POETRY

Copper Canyon Press poets are at the center of all our efforts as a nonprofit publisher. Poets create the art of our books, and they read and teach the books we publish. Many are also generous donors who believe in financially supporting the vibrant poetry community of Copper Canyon Press. For decades, our poets have quietly donated their royalties, have contributed their time to our fundraising campaigns, and have made personal donations in support of emerging and established poets. Their generosity has encouraged the innovative risk-taking that sustains and furthers the art form.

The donor-poets who have contributed to the Press since 2023 include:

Jonathan Aaron
Pamela Alexander
Kazim Ali
Ellen Bass
Erin Belieu
Mark Bibbins
Linda Bierds
Sherwin Bitsui
Jaswinder Bolina
Marianne Boruch
Laure-Anne Bosselaar
Cyrus Cassells
Peter Cole and Adina Hoffman
Elizabeth J. Coleman
Shangyang Fang
John Freeman
Forrest Gander
Jenny George
Dan Gerber
Jorie Graham
Roger Greenwald
Robert and Carolyn Hedin
Bob Hicok
Ha Jin
The estate of Jaan Kaplinski
Laura Kasischke
Jennifer L. Knox
Ted Kooser
Stephen Kuusisto
Deborah Landau
Sung-Il Lee
Ben Lerner
Dana Levin
Maurice Manning
Heather McHugh
Jane Miller
Roger Mitchell
Lisa Olstein
Gregory Orr
Eric Pankey
Kevin Prufer
Alicia Rabins
Dean Rader
Paisley Rekdal
James Richardson
Alberto Ríos
David Romtvedt
Sarah Ruhl
Kelli Russell Agodon
Natalie Shapero
Arthur Sze
Yuki Tanaka
Elaine Terranova
Chase Twichell
Ocean Vuong
Connie Wanek
Emily Warn

Poetry is vital to language and living. Since 1972, Copper Canyon Press has published extraordinary poetry from around the world to engage the imaginations and intellects of readers, writers, booksellers, librarians, teachers, students, and donors.

We are grateful for the major support provided by:

academy of american poets

THE PAUL G. ALLEN FAMILY FOUNDATION

National Endowment for the Arts
arts.gov

To learn more about underwriting
Copper Canyon Press titles,
please call 360-385-4925 ext. 105

We are grateful for the major support provided by:

Anonymous
Jill Baker and Jeffrey Bishop
Anne and Geoffrey Barker
Donna Bellew
Lisha Bian
Will Blythe
John Branch
Diana Broze
John R. Cahill
Sarah J. Cavanaugh
Keith Cowan and Linda Walsh
Peter Currie
Geralyn White Dreyfous
The Evans Family
Mimi Gardner Gates
Gull Industries Inc.
  on behalf of William True
Carolyn and Robert Hedin
David and Jane Hibbard
Bruce S. Kahn
Phil Kovacevich and Eric Wechsler
Maureen Lee and Mark Busto
Ellie Mathews and Carl Youngmann
  as The North Press
Larry Mawby and Lois Bahle
Petunia Charitable Fund and
  adviser Elizabeth Hebert
Suzanne Rapp and Mark Hamilton
Adam and Lynn Rauch
Emily and Dan Raymond
Joseph C. Roberts
Cynthia Sears
Kim and Jeff Seely
Tree Swenson
Julia Sze
Barbara and Charles Wright
In honor of C.D. Wright
  from Forrest Gander
Caleb Young as C. Young Creative
The dedicated interns and faithful
  volunteers of Copper Canyon Press

The pressmark for Copper Canyon Press
suggests entrance, connection, and interaction
while holding at its center
an attentive, dynamic space for poetry.

This book is set in Adobe Garamond Pro.
Book design by Gopa & Ted2, Inc.
Printed on archival-quality paper.